THE DREAMS
BEHIND THE LIES
WE LIVE BY

Hippolyte Flandrin

THE DREAMS
BEHIND THE LIES
WE LIVE BY

❧

Poems

THE DREAMS BEHIND THE LIES WE LIVE BY

Cover Design by Neil Shigley

Interior Design by RMKHOURY

Images by Hippolyte Flandrin

Type is Mercury

Printed in the United States of America

ISBN: 1497472474
ISBN 13: 9781497472471
Library of Congress Control Number: 2014906174
CreateSpace Independent Publishing Platform
North Charleston, South Carolina

The quotation is the death of his beloved Socrates from Plato's "Phaedo"

To Joan Khoury for the Who, When, and Where.
+
To Brent Kubasta for the How and the Why.

CONTENTS

❧❦

THE DREAMS BEHIND THE LIES WE LIVE BY

❧❦

HIPPOLYTE FLANDRIN

THE POETRY OF
HIPPOLYTE FLANDRIN

This Is An Introduction
and
This Is Not An Introduction

కావ్సా

Perhaps this book can be understood and appreciated only by
someone with the same deeply held need to make one's mind
public. It shows, I believe, that consciousness is a tightrope
stretched between two profound thoughts – the despair of truth
and the joy of illusion – a tightrope stretched over the ideas
we live by. Thus, it is neither an instruction book
nor is its purpose to show things as they are rather than as
the world wishes them to be. Indeed, such a book would
annihilate all other books and social life as we know it probably
would cease to exist. No, the whole promise of this book
will be achieved if one person looks inside it and experiences my
uncreated thoughts before they have been expressed.
For it is the witchcraft of language and the iron cage of logic that
turn thoughts worthy of thinking into ideas not
worthy of speaking. It therefore deals with everything
one has a right to expect from the poet and her poetry –
with clarity and with compulsion – to show the
thoughts that cannot be said. For this work to have any value,
I put in only the true stuff. In these lines, you will find no
deception but self deception and its whole sense
may be summarized in these words: I have nothing to say.

Hippolyte Flandrin

0

"Up till this time most of us had been fairly successful
in keeping back our tears;
but when we saw that he was drinking,
that he had actually drunk it,
we could do so no longer;
in spite of myself the tears came pouring out,
so that I covered my face and wept broken-heartedly—
not for him,
but for my own calamity in losing such a friend."

This Message Has No Content

The purpose of the photographs you are about to see
is not to think about them. No, the purpose is to think about
thinking about them. For when you can think about thinking
about them, then your mind will be ready to do poetry.
That is their purpose and the secret of poetry.

HP

THE DREAMS
BEHIND THE LIES
WE LIVE BY

WHY DO WE STILL HAVE MOUNTAINS?

Why do we still have mountains?
They are so difficult to climb.
But what is free is not worth very much to me,
and a tree is known by its fruit.

Why do we still have friendships?
They are so difficult to keep.
But there is more to me than love and indifference,
and life is best lived in the margins.

Why do we still build statues?
They are so difficult to please.
But my hand is more than the sum of its fingers,
and I am the man who woke up.

Why do we still have dreams?
They are so difficult to touch.
But all things are measured against my being,
and my being is measured against nothingness.

Why do we still have mountains?
This stone is so difficult to push.
But a rolling stone is safe,
and that is not what stones are for.

THIS IS THE END

We need to talk, then,
You and I.

This is the end of the world and I alone can stop it. There are rich people without drivers who want to shop and cannot find a parking space at the mall. But, Baby, can you spare 50 cents a day to save the children? You believe that 4 + 12 = 51, believe also in me. I am an educated man with college degrees piled high and deep.

This is the end of the world and I alone can save it. There are too many dogs chasing too few dog biscuits. But, Baby, I was born blind and now I can see myself on TV. You believe in women without men, believe also in me. I have autographed copies of every book written by Jesus.

This is the end of the world and I alone can redeem it. There are no programs to help a blind man find his car after dark. But, Baby, I love books because they make me sleepy. You believe that God created fossils, believe also in me. I have solved human behavior.

This is the end and you must stop trying to improve yourself. Because, Baby, the thing that needs the improving and the thing that does the improving are one and the same thing. Stop wasting your time and my money.

This is the end and you must stop trying to improve the world. Because, Baby, bad things happen to good people and good things happen to bad people. Stop crying and drop your spare change in the cup before I am late for an important meeting with my financial advisor.

This is the end and you must stop trying to improve me. Because, Baby, the things you want to hear cannot be said but only shown. Stop asking me to draw them for you.

Baby, I'll change.
Please come back.

O TIME! O LIGHT! O GOD!

\/
0
[]
-
;
,
:
.

TIME WILL NOT LET ME

Thank you for taking me back to the Sixties,
me and Phyllis driving the drag in my old '59 Ford,
a ten cent Coke, thirty cent gas, and AM radio.
Thanks a lot, Phyllis, for dumping me for that older guy,
instead of waiting for me to finish college like you
promised.

After she dumped you, Phyllis and I dated for two years.
All she ever talked about was how you were the lost love
of her life.
So we broke up.
She got hooked on Wild Turkey and spent six months in
rehab.
Then her mom made her leave town. She bought some
baby shoes,
but she didn't need them.
Now she lives in San Diego with a homeless guy called
Bill,
sleeping in Balboa Park, and Subway when it rains.

You're talking about my tranny friend, Phillip.
Three years ago, before she went through the change,
she was working the carny circuit with some cheap
European circus.
She was the bearded lady and all those steroids made her
very convincing.

When I met Phillip ten months ago,
he was turning tricks in the Tenderloin in San Francisco
with me. We are pretty happy now.
We got daddies.
Life has not been kind to Phillip,
but he loved you both.

THANK YOU, I AM DEEPLY FLAWED

Thank you,
I am deeply flawed.
I know.
It is hard for me and for everyone else.
I want to escape.
But I am free.
So escape is impossible.
That's my mother.
She used to be real pretty.
I feel sorry for her.
She had a failure for a daughter.
I bought some baby shoes.
They were real pretty.
But I didn't use them.
So mom gave them away.
My Robert used to carry me on his shoulders.
He wanted to change the world for me.
But I am old.
And the world is still the same.
Tell them I've had a wonderful life.

CLING AND WAIT

I love you like an eye and its field of vision.
You and I are an illusion created by an illusionist to
embrace an illusion of love.
We cling to the foot of the Cross, and wait.
We cling to what we used to be, and wait.
We cling to the silence between our words, and wait.
I don't know which came first, but I'm pretty sure God
did not sit on an egg.

I love you like my hand and the word hand.
You and I are not who we think we are, but who I think
you think we are and who you think I think we are.
We cling to the other that is no longer the other, and
wait.
We cling to an escape that is hidden by familiarity, and
wait.
We cling to a world bounded in a nutshell, and wait.
I don't know why we are here, but I'm pretty sure we are
two strangers trying to walk each other home.

YOU FOUND ME IN THE CLOSET

You found me in the closet hiding an unborn child that
made me complete,
like a martyr without a cross.
And you said,
It is better not to love than to have loved and lost.

You found me in the bedroom kissing two sets of
footprints in the sand,
like a thought without words.
And you said,
Live each day as if you will live forever.

You found me in the kitchen sifting the broken bones and
rotting flesh of a withered corpse,
like a patriot without a flag.
And you said,
It is not the strong that survive, but the durable.

You found me in the garage measuring pictures at an
exhibition of dreams,
like a hurt without a disease.
And you said,
Lack of communication is the key to a successful
marriage.

THE FOUR SEASONS

Spring is my favorite season.
It is a tightrope stretched across an abyss between a
thing and a thing-in-itself.
It is an answered prayer crucified by faith and
resurrected by doubt.
It is a birthday party for a truth celebrated by
exaggerations and falsehoods.
Spring is a snail on a basketball.

Winter is my favorite season.
It is an idea inside a thought inside a word inside an
emotion.
It is a choice between the way of what is and the way of
what is not.
It is a wedding between the called and the chosen
celebrated by hypocrites.
Winter is a foot hiding from a shoe.

Fall is my favorite season.
It is heading down a dead-end street and knowing where
it leads.
It is climbing to the end of a rope and finding a noose.
It is a love affair between a movie star and a leper
celebrated by the usual gang of idiots.
Fall is my boyfriend's hands on my shoulders for no
reason.

Summer is my favorite season.
It is a single mom with a baby that didn't patch things up between us.
It is hugging my mom and she doesn't let go first.
It is a funeral for a cynic mourned by a skeptic.
Summer is a joke about a bowling ball, a messiah, and a pitchfork.

DECEIT IS A BLIND FALLING FORWARD

Deceit is a blind falling forward into my backward arms.
I close my eyes and I see an apple tree curled around a
snake and
I see a wooden cross nailed into a man and
I see a warm grave unwelcome the dead.
Words have consequences that thoughts cannot.
Did you think of me in the lobby with your arm around
her waist?
What did she mean by "stupid cunning"?
Why can I remember the future as clearly as I remember
the past?
Truth has consequences that illusions cannot.
Deceit is feeling your blind hands under my favorite
sweater.
What I see is made out of things which do not appear.

MONEY IS EVIL BUT I LIKE IT

Money is evil but I like it.
Since I met you, I am always alone, but never lonely.
I smelled her perfume in your hair and didn't cry.
When you are not with me, I imagine you are.
When you are, I imagine you are with her.
When you are with her, I imagine a rock too big to lift
and I lift it.
I committed a sin in which I forgive you.
Since I am a habit that became a convenience.
You are a convenience that became a necessity.
Money is a secure refuge in life, but, above all, in death.

HELEN, GEORGIA

I blah, therefore, blah blah.
Genuine imitation hand embroidered deer antler
funnel cake,
Genuine simulated hand blown bear skin lipstick case,
Genuine synthetic hand carved milk chocolate music
box.
He is making a list on his Harley and checking it twice
for wine stains.

Our father who blah blah blahblah.
Genuine imitation beer fudge earrings,
Genuine simulated pecan fried sauerkraut,
Genuine synthetic biscuit churned leather.
He is going to find out who has been a naughty sausage
or a nice cream puff.

DASEIN

We can never know what we want,
but we can know what we don't want,
and what we don't want is what we do know.
Many are thawed,
but few are frozen.

We can never taste the difference between a real apple
pie and an unreal apple pie,
but my girlfriend knows a contradiction from a tautology,
and what is is real that is real is-ness.
Saints die daily,
but I die hourly.

We can never know why we are here,
but we can know that we are alone,
and what poetry there can be after gods by the dozens
fall like movie stars from the heavens.
I was born in an iron cage of luxurious filth and
miserable ease,
but two roads diverged and I chose meaninglessness,
and that has made all the difference.

We can never escape from a room with no exit,
but we can know two, maybe three dozen bartenders by
name,
and my guilt is in the choosing and not the choice.
I listened to the dull and ignorant,
and they, too, have their story,
but when they cried,
I could only cry with them.

RAY MANZAREK, 1939-2013

My thoughts fly up, my words stay below.
Thoughts without words are like windows without glass
and doors without locks.
When is a door not a door, John?
When it jerks me out of myself, like a jar falling off
a shelf.

I said, Jim, if the whole carpet is green, then every
thread is green.
You said, your whole is less than the sum of my parts.
I was playing a part and didn't know it, pretending to be
someone else.
Someone you could love without hope, someone you
could forget without guilt.

You go through my house like a mannequin born blind,
littering emotions on the sidewalk above my bed.
Do you remember how Robby didn't want to let go?
Why didn't you stop me from clinging to you in a
changing world,
and washing your clothes with my own?
It is not enough to be strong, you said, my clothes must
be durable.

DIOGENES, 412-323

Perhaps it is better to judge a means by its ends rather
than a cover by its book.
Perhaps great Alexander will give me a fish rather than
teach me how to fish in a barrel.

Remember washing vegetables in the river with me and
cupping our hands to drink from them?
Remember how sweet and clean the waterness tasted in
the cupness of our handness?

I searched an empty crowd for a human being and
pleasured myself in a popular shopping mall.
I searched an empty mind for a kingdom of dogs and
relieved myself on the chariots of kings.

Pleasure, wealth, fame, and power,
what I cannot get enough of.
Unattainable, unfulfilling, insatiable, and fleeting,
what I do not really want.

Son, you must look forward so you don't bump into
things.
Dad, I walk backward so I can understand where I have
been.
To him, love is mutually assured disappointment.
To me, hatred will never cease.

THE MEANING OF LIFE

A flower means this.
A bee means that.
No bees, no flowers.
No flowers, no bees.
But I am not this, not that.

A noun means this.
A verb means that.
No nouns, no verbs.
No verbs, no nouns.
But I am not this, not that.

A word means this.
A thought means that.
No words, no thoughts.
No thoughts, no words.
But I am not this, not that.

I went out of my mind.
I came to my senses.
I was cured by words.
I was bewitched by language.
But I am neither the alpha nor the omega.

I am a thing inside a void.
I am a void inside a thing.
I am a little man inside my head.
I am a wave inside an infinite ocean.
But I am neither the car nor the driver.

I cannot see the I that sees me.
I cannot drown twice in the same river.
I cannot doubt that I doubt.
I cannot cling to the clinging.
But I am neither a creator nor a creation.
Simply I simply am.

MOTHER'S DAY

Do you remember when I wrote my name for the first
time?
I remember you staying out too late with your friends
and finding you passed out in the front yard again.

Do you remember when bad things happened to good
people?
I remember you running to tell me first.

Do you remember when I chose the happiness of illusion
rather than the despair of truth?
I remember you selling a brand new pair of baby shoes.

Do you remember when I couldn't stop crying and you
cried with me?
I remember begging bartenders not to serve you.

Do you remember when I got sunburned playing at the
beach?
I remember rubbing cold cream on your back until you
fell asleep.

MARSHA KROFCHIK, 1951-2000

In 63 I was 12 and the continent of Atlantis was an
island, before the terrible flood, that sat at her desk
across the room in the area we now call the Atlantic
Ocean. So great an island, that Mrs. Tenpenny asked her
to choose her best friend. She looked at me for the first
time and smiled. She had a smile that could kill North
Vietnam. Knowing her fate, Atlantis sent heavenly ships
filled with contradictions, exaggerations, uncritical
assumptions, and total falsehoods to all four corners of
the world. On board were the 12 bartenders speaking
with one voice:
"I want my real mother,
I want my real father,
Have mercy on me."
Marsha got drunk last night in noble silence, crossed
herself, and glided into a speeding car. The dead are
indeed a better neighborhood.

MEDITATION ON HOMELESS BILL

Bill Randall or Bill Murphy follows yesterday's stars
to Pantoja Park, where Jesus parked 12 Cadillacs in 11
parking spaces.

Bill Randall or Bill Murphy sleeps under the table in
Starbucks to escape an avalanche of cats and dogs,
where Jesus served brides and grooms on Christmas
morning turning stale coffee into wine.

Bill Randall or Bill Murphy stands and falls on a
cement block cheering deaf and dumb baseball through
a painful window, where good angels ascended and
descended on the battered body of Christ as he walked
to home plate.

Bill Randall or Bill Murphy buys a blessed beer now and
then with his buddies Washington and Jefferson who
sleep in a paper cup at the Hyatt, where a stoned, empty
Jesus picked up the Easter bunny waitressing in the bar
on a long weekend in Hell.

Bill Randall or Bill Murphy carries his home in two
holy grocery bags from Ralphs's market, where Jesus
awakened his buddy Lazarus who was sleeping like a
baby in the meat department.

ARGUMENTUM AD HOMINEM

What if Hitler wrote the Bible?
Things are not what we wish them to be.
Things are not what we imagine them to be.
Things are what they are.
Every day I drag my illusions across the floor from my
bed to a chair near one small window,
and every night you drag them back.

Why do situations unfold regardless of how we feel about
them?
Either it is day or it is night.
Either you are an ass or not an ass.
Either this thing is within our control or it is not.
Every day I wait for you in the parking lot outside a
casino,
and every night they drag you back.

Where are all of the Jesuses Jesus promised us?
I love you, but I cannot empty my thoughts into your
mind.
I love you, but I cannot teach you how to make me happy.
I love you, but I cannot teach algebra to a dog.
Every day I cut out my heart with my teeth,
and every night my heart grows back.

Am I a real person living a real life in a real world?
How can I live a happy life without you?
How can you become a better person with me?
How can I stop my hopes and fears from swaying me
against you?
Every day I smother you to death with a satin pillow,
and every night I feel your breath on the back of my
neck.

MY BELLY IS TORMENTED

My belly is tormented by perpetual vultures,
Loyal vultures with baby faces telling secrets,
Public secrets about you behind my back.

The newspaper said tragedy strikes blind woman after
her dog ran away and was adopted by another family.
I ate bread over your chest and drank wine over your
body and you blinded me.

I hold my breath until my head is about to explode.
I feel my eyes sinking like stones in a deep well.
I do not know where I belong but it is neither where
I have been nor where I am going.

The newspaper said tragedy strikes family of four in
mine shaft explosion.
I waited four hours for you before I walked home with
the bartender.

KINGDOM OF DOUBT

Kingdom of Doubt:
left-handed monster,
pauperizer of perfect happiness,
imitator of infinite wisdom,
three sparrows landed at my feet and feasted on the
crumbs that fell from my table,
and is there no one who understands me?

Kingdom of Falsehood:
two-tongued jackalope,
hypocrisy's flag unfurled,
ego's wish unfulfilled,
three lions studied a painting of a hunter killing a lion
and feasted on the flesh of the artist,
and are the limits of my lies then the limits of my world?

Kingdom of Appearances:
green-tailored envy,
unravished bride of the unperceived,
permanent guide to the perplexed,
three orphans walked into a bar and said in one voice,
and can you feast on the memories of your father and
your mother and be worthy of me?

EITHER/OR

What incessantly varying recurring themes drive
history like a red truck and drive me?

Why do perpetual spirit, mind, will, and being push
someone like you into my bedroom countless times on a
star and push me?

When shall I see a red wheel of severed heads and touch
their shadows on the cave wall and hear them toll with
one voice and know it tolls for me?

Who am I, then, if I am more than one name called for
me and one face traced for me and one mind measured
for me and one world staged for me and one part fitted
for me?

Where can I find two or more of you gathered together
in my name and break this endless cycle of birth and
death that makes me both/either desire and/or despise
you?

GOD EXISTS

Killer tornado destroys only Atlanta adult bookstores,
whorehouses, and topless bars but all churches, mosques,
and synagogues are untouched:
God's righteousness requires that the faithful sheep will
be rewarded and the evil goats punished.

Killer tornado destroys only Atlanta churches, mosques,
and synagogues but all adult bookstores, whorehouses,
and topless bars are untouched:
God's mysterious ways and inscrutable wisdom require
that sometimes bad things must happen to good people
and good things happen to bad people.

Killer tornado destroys only that blonde girl you touched
on the cheek outside the movie theater where I followed
you:
God's plan requires that yes, I'm sure you are the father
of my unborn child and no, I won't get rid of it because
it's my problem.

THE SWIMMER

Is there no end to deceiving oneself?
Is it prudent for the pompous pilot to fly unborn children
to heaven?
Is there a clever swimmer among us who can swim twice
in the same river?
Why is climbing to the foot of the cross like a sinful
donkey climbing a ladder?
The ladder can be kicked away once the donkey reaches
the top.

Is it stupid cunning that leavens too many lies with too
little truth?
Is the phony world made whole every moment complete
with our phony memories of the past?
Is the swimmer damned who acquits the guilty?
Why does it take three apostles to perform an abortion?
One to hold the abortion and two to turn the ladder.

Is it safe to tightly wrap lies in the Holy Bible before
freezing them for winter?
Is every mind filled with two pictures: the me I am and
the me I am not?
Is there any difference between the unseen swimmer
and the swimmer who does not exist?
Why did Jesus cross the road?
He could not choose to do otherwise in the same
situation.

THEME FOR AN IMAGINARY NEWSPAPER ON JUNE 3

June is the best month for bears. My wife loved animals. She rescued her bulldog, Pumpkin. She was so pretty. Cancer ate her to the bone. Tell them I've had a wonderful life, she said. Investors have lost momentum. Defensive stocks are getting hit hardest. I promised myself to change the world for her. But she is gone and the world is still the same. Uncertainty over the price of oil is driving down bond yields. So I raced up and down the stairs hoping to have a heart attack. We have no children. I hated my father and never wanted to be one. Sometimes, there is more than one right answer. But sometimes, there is none. Stocks, with their potential for higher returns, have been the best place to invest money in a high unemployment world. What would Jesus do if she asked him to help her have an abortion? He would help her. A rapid rise in interest rates could slow the economic recovery as investors start selling bonds ahead of a pullback in stock prices. Unborn Baby Shoes. Like New. Best Offer. What is a clinging man to do in a changing world? There is a grief that once entered, we refuse to exit. The stock market, which has finished up seven months in a row, may have you kicking yourself for taking chips off the table. There are some mistakes we can never stop paying for. All we can do is to cling and wait. The Dow fell 209 points on Friday.

FREE WILL IN THE SOCIAL WORLD

I. One can mistreat anybody that one will never meet again.
Dentists are more real than cab drivers.
Waitresses are not as human as elevator operators.
All mothers exist but no fathers.
Being there is more than being as a dog is more loyal than a toothbrush.

II. One can kill rather than risk thinking an original thought.
It is better to build a prison than to boil a hotdog.
Hearing is better than listening as a dead Moslem is better than a good Moslem.
Adultery is between one man and one woman.
I met three hermits walking on water and told them to get a job.

III. One must have a span of sympathy in order to be a good person.
A starving baby in Africa is not as hungry as the one in my front yard.
A man who beats his wife is to a man who beats his dog as a pedicure is to a double mastectomy.
A mother had four children and sold two of them: How many children did she have?
My boyfriend and I promised to hold on to each other forever but our arms tired and we let go.

WHO IS MY NEIGHBOR?

Who is my neighbor but one that is not-this and
not-that?:
It is a messenger of freedom with disorder and control
without freedom;
It is a wall uniting the joy of illusion and the despair of
truth;
It is a man burning in flames who cannot wake up and a
man walking on water who woke up;
It is an umbrella neither for raining nor not raining.

As Santa delivers toys;
As storks deliver babies;
As automobiles deliver pizza;
As Jesus delivers puppies:
Who is my neighbor but one that is seen but not heard,
heard but not touched, and touched but not seen?

Who is my neighbor but one that is indifferent in love,
committed in deceit, and confirmed in doubt?:
I built a fence between me and my neighbor and we
became friends;
I built a door between me and my neighbor and we
became strangers;
I built a prison for me and my neighbor and we were
safe;
I built a church for me and my neighbor and we
went mad.

THE LORD'S PRAYER

Our father, not biologically but machine-ghostly, who
I know not as a justified true belief is in heaven, a real
place in outer space but not a sense-experience that we
can empirically see, feel, hear, smell, or taste, hallowed
be your name that varies wildly according to one's native
language. Your kingdom come down to the empirical
world below, your all-powerful will be in control without
freedom rather than our free will with the risk of
disorder, on earth as it is in heaven where your home is
when you are not visiting us. Give us today all of the stuff
we need to be happy without regard to culture, values,
norms, mores, and folkways, and forgive us our mistakes
and blunders that hurt other people because we forgive
people who hurt us and you are a lot better person than
we are. And do not let bad things happen to good people
or good things happen to bad people, but give good
things to good people and bad things to bad people. For
everything in heaven and earth is your private property,
and legally, morally, ethically, spiritually, physically,
positively, absolutely, undeniably and reliably you can do
as you please, so please, do things my way.

ANATOMY OF A FRIENDSHIP

There are good friends and bad friends as there are good
dentists and bad dentists.
It is a job like any other with rewards and expenses.
I do favors for my friend, John.
These are my expenses.
My friend, John, does favors for me.
These are my rewards.
Subtract my expenses from my rewards and the result is
the total value of our friendship.
If our friendship has a positive value, then John is a good
friend.
If our friendship has a negative value, then John is a bad
friend.
A good friendship deserves to be nurtured.
A bad friendship must be terminated.
John should have known these things before he
refused me.
For a refusal is not the act of a friend.
And why I turned my back on him.
Poor John, I said, our friendship does not have a positive
value and forgiveness is an expense.
Nothing is so tragic as arithmetic.

MEDITATION ON THE RUDE AND INCONVENIENT DEATH OF MY BEST FRIEND

We so loved the moon that we denied our only begotten
sun of the soothing touch of a human hand,
and behaved as if we would live forever in the shadows
that know the smiling face behind the smiling mask.
When we did bad things, we confessed to the darkness
but sacrificed to the light,
and behaved as if we were born together but could only
die alone.
We so loved looking backward that we denied living
forward,
and behaved as if our youth was nailed to a wall with
500 bottles of beer.
When there was trouble, I looked behind me to see if
they were there,
and behaved as if I knew damn'd well they were.
We so loved remembering the past that we denied
remembering the future,
and behaved as if we lived on the back of a half-distance
turtle that is one inch from a wall and never arrives.
When I once dreamed that I had ceased to be, I see my
friends laughing over me and hear them speaking in one
voice, "He filled a much needed void in our lives,"
and behaved as if the first to go is blessed, who will never
see the others go before him.

MY FRAGMENT OF INSIGHT

You are like the damn ocean.
You wash over the damn seashore and devour it.
You leave behind imaginary things I cannot get enough
of but do not really want.
You take nothing with you when you leave again but
missing pieces of me.
You always return them when I forget you have them
and bring more of your damn things.
You fill my soul with your damn things.
You should leave your damn key or I should change the
damn lock.
You said a damn baby would patch things up between us.
You said a damn baby would bring us closer together.
You said things that were true in my mind but not in
the vat.
You hurt me.
You cheat me.
You abuse me.
For you, my need will never end.

NOTES ON FRIENDSHIP BY PETER CUSHING AND CHRISTOPHER LEE

We have in our life one and only one friend,
a friend whom you love with all your heart and care for
very much,
so very much that you are able to trust your one true self
only to him,
and when he has been separated from you by the clock or
the compass you know,
you just know from his very first laugh who you are and
who he is,
and when he is gone you smile for him but weep for
yourself that nothing like him will happen to your life
ever again.

Now he is gone,
gone and I cannot find,
find what I am looking for.
For my heart is empty,
empty of everything.
Everything is killing time.
Time does not keep me alive now.
Now my only ambition is someday,
someday I will join my dear friend and we will be
reunited.

ON FIRST LOOKING INTO DASS'S BE HERE NOW

Much have I traveled in the realms of golf,
and many good memories of the past have I seen,
and some of them may be true,
and being born and knowing only life,
and knowing nothing and being certain of everything,
I pledged my allegiance to the flag of my unfulfilled
desires.

But I never understood the true meaning of Christmas
until Ram Dass ate two forbidden biscuits from the tree
of knowledge,
and then in the private luggage of my mind,
and under the water where Jesus walked,
and around the lions at the gates of perfect wisdom,
and over the rainbow of infinite happiness,
I saw that who I am is behind all of it sitting silent on a
moving mountain peak.

But I hit myself on the head and heard a hollow sound,
and freedom is like a middle finger pointed at the moon,
and the power of reason is like a beautiful whore who
handcuffed me to the bed and stole my wallet,
and the faith of our fathers is like a beautiful whore who
married me and gave birth to seven men without women,
and power over all things is like an angel who carried me
to heaven and gave me a job cleaning dirty windshields
at stop lights,

I found that freedom is knowing that there are no known
unknowns that I am conscious of or unknown unknowns
that I am unconscious of but only knowns that litter the
mind of God like empty beer bottles on a beach.

Much of what I eat is what I am as the structures of the
world have become the structures of my mind,
and that is how I blessed a barren fig tree,
and how I made lemons from lemonade,
and how I called Peter to come to me and smiled as his
sinking fear drowned him,
and how I placed the mountain there so there the
mountain stayed,
I looked in the eyes of my illusion of myself and asked
her to loan me twenty dollars.

ON LUDWIG WITTGENSTEIN

Yes, I was in my favorite bookstore reading a magazine article about a man who calmly walked into a police station. Then he handed a note to a cop, "I am God. Please help me."

No, every human being must make a profound choice between two indisputably undesirable, but nevertheless, clearly distinguishable futures: To be happy and incompetent like an airplane pilot or to be competent and unhappy like a philosopher. Then I asked my ex-husband about the blessed fruit of my womb and you said, "I have nothing to say."

Maybe, what is unsaid is more important than what is said. You said, "I love you." I think that means, "I love you forever." But language is silence's fool. It means, "I love you now."

Yes, Mary had a little lamb. Mary ate the lamb? Mary owned the lamb? Mary had sexual relations with the lamb? Mary gave birth to the lamb? You held my head between your hands and said, "Mary didn't want to see and she still is not seeing it."

No, I love my baby. I love pie. I love crossword puzzles. I love my mother. I love his hands on my shoulders. If there was a pill that could change the way I am, I would take it. But you laughed, "The word is a memory. And a memory can mean anything one wants it to mean."

Maybe, we were perfect for each other: I expected too much and you didn't expect enough. I tore a page from the magazine and put it in my pocket when the cashier was busy. My eyes filled with tears as I whispered to myself, "No, no, no, no, no."

ON ALAN WATTS

Why is something better than nothing?
See the piece of paper you are holding.
See the little black marks.
See the white spaces surrounding the black marks.
See the black marks without the white spaces.
See the white spaces without the black marks.

Why are the black marks more important than the white
spaces?
See black without white.
See that black without white is blind.
See white without black.
See that white without black is blind.
See that white is black and black is white.

Why is good good and evil evil?
See the world.
See the good.
The good is good.
See the evil.
The evil is evil.
See the world without the good.
See the world without the evil.
See the window.
See the glass.
The glass is good.
See the wooden frame.
The frame is evil.
See the window without the frame.
See the window without the glass.

See the human body.
See the head.
The head is good.
See the feet.
The feet are evil.
See the body without the head.
See the body without the feet.

Why are winners cheered and losers booed?
See the race.
See winners and losers.
See how different they look.
Hooray winners!
Boo losers!
See winners without losers.
See losers without winners.
See bees and flowers.
See how different they look.
Hooray flowers!
Boo bees!
See flowers without bees.
See bees without flowers.
See the ocean and the wave.
See how different they look.
Boo ocean!
Hooray wave!
See the ocean without the wave.
See the wave without the ocean.

What does it mean to perfect the world?
See the world.
See that the world needs improvement.

See that the world needs more somethingness than
nothingness.
See that the world needs more black than white.
See that the world needs more good than evil.
See that the world needs more hoorays than boos.

DECONSTRUCTION

I told him that when we made love I couldn't tell if
he was thinking of me or his wife. He said, "It's not
important that you know, only that I know."

I told him that I would be happy to help wash his dishes
and fold his clothes. He said, "I have always paid cash for
true love and I always will."

I told him to tell me how much he loves me. He said,
"When a woman like you asks for a commitment she
is overestimating the value of what she must have and
underestimating the value of what she must give up."

I told him that I was certain it is his baby. He said,
"A baby begins with wonder and ends with doubt."

I told him that I couldn't live without him. He said,
"A dinosaur walked into a psychiatrist's office and said,
'Please help me. I'm madly in love with a married man.'
And the psychiatrist replies, 'If you love him, you must
have an abortion.'"

I told him that we will be a real family. He said, "Family
means treating me as a means to an end and never again
as an end in itself."

ALL SECRETS HIDE SINS

I read the news in a train.
The American government is spying on Americans.
Spying on Americans to learn all of our secrets.
All secrets hide sins.
Sins that threaten.
Threaten to make us pay for our secrets.
I said, "Can an all-powerful God create a rock so big that
even He cannot lift it?"
X said, "I have nothing to say."

I read the news in a car.
Nothing is right if it is done by a thousand women.
All women should have wives.
But no men.
Nothing is wrong if it is done by a thousand men.
All men should have husbands.
But no women.
I said, "A pat on its head will make a dog wag its tail.
What will a goose do?"
X said, "It will make him wonder."

I read the news in outer space.
Spying keeps Americans safe.
Safe from attack by our enemies.
And our enemies never again attacked us.
I said, "Three wrongs make a right."
X said, "The only difference between good and evil is
that evil has red hair."

I read the news in a plane.
First the Fasten Seat Belt sign is turned on.
And then the ride gets bumpy.
So X asked the pilot to stop turning the sign on.
And the ride never again was bumpy.
I said, "If I had ten minutes left to live I would spend it
strangling you to death."
X said, "At least I won't die alone."

ARLINGTON

If you care to think about it, there are more headstones
than there ought to be.
With a war of coincidence in Spain here, and a war of
choice in Vietnam there.
Here a war of stupidity in Iraq, there a war of vengeance
in Afghanistan, everywhere a fool's war.
Row after row of white picket fences crowding in honor
and crowding out hope.
Column after column of black dotted dominoes tumbling
forward to glory and tumbling backward to oblivion.
What is red and white and blue and full of holes?
A hole is less than the sum of its parts.

If you care to think about it, they gave their lives to make
the world safe for shopping.
General Electric said, "War is sell."
General Motors said, "I shall return with receipt."
Row after row of great novels that will never be written
and great diseases that will never be cured.
Column after column of girls that will never fall in love
and boys that will never be cool.
What grows in size as you remove more and more
from it?
Colonel Sanders said, "A grave is a soldier under a helmet
under the sand under a bikini."

HUMAN BEHAVIOR HAS BEEN SOLVED

I once loved my father and my mother and they
loved me,
but a good life is a good triangle,
and I must keep my triangle in balance,
so as my mother grew to despise my father,
so I turned my back on my father that I love,
and I could not speak to him for the last 17 years of his
life,
because two negatives and one positive is a balanced
triangle,
and a balanced triangle is a good life.

I once loved my husband and my unborn baby and they
loved me,
but a bad triangle is a bad life,
and a hell of infinite freedom,
so as my husband grew to fear my child,
so I turned against my baby that I love,
and got rid of it one sunny morning after a big breakfast
of blueberry pancakes and extra bacon,
because I refused to be convicted of freedom and
condemned to choose.

I once loved my trash baby and myself and they
loved me,
but an unbalanced triangle is filled with perfect remorse
and ultimate self-deception,
so as my baby grew to hate me,

so I turned indifferent to myself that I love,
and went home after lunch one sunny afternoon and
opened my wrists,
because where there is no choice, there can be no guilt,
but only grace and redemption.

THE PERSISTENCE OF AGGREGATES AND THE INSTINCT FOR COMBINATIONS

Your father taught you that the best way of doing something is the way it has always been done.

If you want to change a lightbulb, then you ask yourself, "How would my father change a lightbulb?", and you do it the same way.

If you want to betray your pregnant wife, then you ask yourself, "How would my father betray his pregnant wife?", and you do it the same way.

If you want to fuck my best friend in my bedroom, then you ask yourself, "How would my father fuck his wife's best friend in his wife's bedroom?", and you do it the same way.

If you want to look into my eyes and lie to my face like a selfish pig, then you ask yourself, "How would my father look in his wife's eyes and lie to her face like a self-centered pig?", and you do it the same way.

"I pledge allegiance to the persistence of aggregates and to self-deception for which it stands, one right way under my father's eyes hypocritical with rule-following and role-playing for all, forever and ever. Amen."

My mother taught me that the new is synonymous with the best.

New people are better than old people.
New sex is better than old sex.
New vaginas are better than old vaginas.
New babies are better than old babies.
New wives are better than old wives.
New whores are better than old whores.

"Our instinct for combinations. Thy conclusions come.
Thy morning after pill be done on my guilt as it is in my
belly. Give us this day our daily miscarriage and forgive
him his tight pussies. So help me, Bill."

WHORE

He treats me like his high school sweetheart.
Shy.
Eager.
Cute.
Maybe thirty.
A doctor of some kind.
His thing is to take me to his apartment and make me
wear a fancy silk negligee and act like I enjoy it.
Then we do it and I go home.
He pays me in syringes and I let him.

He respects me as someone who makes more an hour
than he does.
Funny.
Sad.
Nervous.
Maybe fifty.
A construction worker.
His thing is to come to my apartment and cook a big
breakfast for us with eggs and bacon and pancakes and
everything.
Then we have sex before we eat it and I go home.
He is missing three fingers on his right hand.

He doesn't feel he is cheating on his wife if she doesn't
know about us.
Kind.
Polite.
Lonely.
Maybe forty.

A schoolteacher.
His thing is that we sleep in the same bed but he doesn't touch me and just wants to cuddle.
Then he shows me pictures of his two kids and I go home.
He put me to bed one night after I drank too much and did embarrassing things and he didn't hit me like I thought he would.

BUM

it has been rough on the street
i worked in construction for twenty years
then i lost my job and my house
i lived in my car but i had to sell it to buy my wife and
daughter a ticket home
my wife used to be real pretty
sometimes i sleep in a flop house on forty third street for
sixteen bucks for twenty four hours
but sometimes i come up dry
so i sleep in cardboard boxes or under bridges
i like sleeping in the park
but the cops chase me away at five in the morning
i apply for jobs
but i dont look like i used to and i smell
so they tell me to leave my phone number and they will
call me
but i dont have a phone like i used to
i stand outside this station every day
i depend on the train people
i show them respect and some people give me leftover
food from nice restaurants
it is humiliating to be shaking a cup all day
but begging gives you humility and you lose your shame
i am glad my little girl cant see me
some people call me names
yesterday a guy in a nice suit walks passed me and says
get a job bum
i say god bless you and he keeps on walking
he walks about a block and then he turns around and
walks back

he says would you accept my apology
he says i had a pretty bad day
then he gives me everything he has in his pocket
about thirty bucks
i add up my cup at the end of the day
sometimes it is pretty dry
i watch people take the train home
i feel so bad that i cant go home
some people look at me like i am nothing but a bum
but i was a human being before i was a bum and i think i
still am

BABY KILLER

This was my abortion:
I was sixteen.
I loved my boyfriend so much.
Now I can't remember his name.
I remember that I was so scared and so ashamed.
I wanted to kill myself but I didn't know how.
We lived in Texas.
My mom and dad told me to quit school because I had no choice.
My school told me that a fetus is a baby like an acorn is an oak tree.
My church told me that a fetus is renting my body and that a tenant has more authority over the house than its owner.
Everyone said that everything was my fault.
I was so confused.
My Uncle Arthur lives in Brooklyn.
I was six when he told me that he is my godfather, and I laughed, "You're not God!"
On my birthday, he still sends me funny checks like $124.51.
He asked me what I wanted to do.
He was with me every second and never let go of my hand.
When it was over, he took me to Coney Island and we rode the Wonder Wheel.
I started to cry and he cried with me.

THE APPEARANCE OF WHAT YOU IS AND WHAT YOU IS LIKE

There is a tiny woman named Roberta inside my head
sitting in a comfortable chair eating popcorn and
watching a television screen showing pictures of my
sense impressions of the external world.
Roberta sees cat images.
Roberta smells cat odor.
Roberta feels cat fur.
Roberta hears cat purring.
But cat properties are all that can ever be experienced by
Roberta and all that Roberta can ever know.
But not the cat-like thing itself.
I cannot tell if what it is like and what it is are one and
the same thing.

There is a tiny woman named Roberta inside my heart
sitting in front of a window and watching the things you
do that make me want you so badly.
Roberta sees love odors.
Roberta smells love images.
Roberta feels love sounds.
Roberta hears love touches.
But love properties are all that Roberta can ever know.
But not the love-like thing itself.
I cannot tell if what you is like and what you is are one
and the same is.
I cannot tell if you are still that man or if you ever were.

THE GUN REPORT

A curious Georgia boy from Rome,
Was shot dead in his grandparent's home,
An accidental discharge hit,
Him in the face with a stray bullet,
And his brother will grow up alone.

Under her bed hiding undefended,
A little girl was not the target intended,
A burglar shot her dead,
With her father's gun he fled,
And no suspects have been apprehended.

A domestic shooting left a mother of four wounded,
In a Dallas residential neighborhood,
Officers arrived too late to save her,
Declared dead a short time later,
And her husband took his own life barricaded.

No one is in custody in St. Louis this night,
Where a man went bike riding with his wife,
He returned home to stifle,
A robber armed with his own rifle,
And now he is clinging to life.

A police officer was shot in the chest, stomach, and head,
Outside a motorcycle club in New Orleans,
Unresponsive when officers arrived,
He died before his pregnant wife could be notified,
And two men and a woman fled the scene.

DOES GOD EXIST?

I have faith in many people which do not appear.
I followed the map and had faith in the mapmaker that I
have never seen.
I learned the history book and believed in the historian
that I have never touched.
I ravished the wisdom of Socrates and trusted in Plato
that I have never heard.
What becomes of those who have stopped saying prayers
but who have not stopped praying?

This is a book.
I am holding it.
I know that it is under my hand.
I do not have faith.
I know.
Where there is no doubt, there can be no faith.

This was my husband.
I was holding him.
I thought that I had him in the palm of my hand.
I should not have followed him.
I know that now.
It is better to live with a lie and be happy than to know
the truth and be disappointed.

I have faith in twenty angels which do not appear.
I know that ten are sleeping and as they sleep they
dream of my marriage as I want it to be.

I know that nine are playing dice with my marriage and
as they play they bet that a baby won't patch things up
between us.
I know that one is whispering something funny about
me to God.
What becomes of those with no one left to lean on but
their doubts?

ARMOR

Armor that is forged by perpetual success and hand-
hammered achievement.
Armor that clings to me like sleep to a dream.
Armor that obscures my deceit with vanity like mud on
a pig.
Armor that shields me from myself like flesh from bone.
Armor that conceals wisdom with virtue as a clock
strangles time with both hands.
Armor that orphans my weaknesses and fathers my
strengths.
Armor that will not free Abraham to know what Lincoln
is doing.
Armor that calls me to my reunion as Siddhartha is
called to the Buddha.
Armor that calls me to be the person I am to fulfill my
wish to love the person I am.
Armor that calls me to fear from safety as a priest is
called to hear his own confession.
Armor that is forged by pleasure, by wealth, by fame, and
by power clouds me as a statue clouds the man.

A MOTHER DOES NOT FORGET

A mother does not forget.
I remember him at three.
He walked to the piano as if he belonged to it.
And he started playing.
And he would not stop.
A mother is proud of her son.
Then he was seventeen.
He performed at Carnegie Hall.
He played for the Pope.
He could have had a wonderful career as a concert
pianist.
A mother knows what is best for her son.
But he wanted to fight for his country.
He enlisted in the Marines.
And deployed to Afghanistan.
During training for his deployment he broke a finger.
A mother prays for her son.
A broken finger would keep him from deploying with his
comrades.
The man on his right and the man on his left.
The doctor said I can treat it and you will not deploy.
Or I can cut it off and you get on the plane.
A mother protects her son.

ON STEVE MCQUEEN

Among the crowds of thick refugees eclipsed by
Hollywood Mammon,
You could spot him in an instant like the joy of despair in
a cathedral,
Sad-eyed orphan blood flowing in his veins but no less
frisky or fool-wise,
Keeper of seven sins and bringer of seven saints,
He made us want to die with him,
Like bullets from the same gun,
No white-hat moralizing, he was a grinning inferno of vices,
No nouns and verbs, he used his eyes like a blind man
uses a cane,
He should have been a priest,
And so a priest he became,
Turning retreat's sweet water into rebellion's sour wine,
He crammed together normlessness and powerlessness
inside meaninglessness,
And so a magician he became,
Turning stones into sand, sand into clay, and clay into
flesh,
He crammed together sin and redemption inside
indifference,
Put this one on a horse to bring the money in,
Put that one on a woman to bring the money in,
Put him on anything and bring in the money,
He would help anyone to escape,
A shepherd who snatched the stray sheep who blew his
way,
And never asked to be embraced by an old man or a
pining young girl.

THERE ARE MORE WORLDS TO SING IN

There are more worlds to sing in, my father said,
Who, in order to be happy, must have his child on his
knee,
Holding my wet face in his rough hands to cover it with
kisses.

There are many ways to turn earthly friendships into
bitterness, my mother said,
Who, in order to have infinite wisdom, must have the
choicest contemplation,
Solving my despair in perfect clarity as a hive bee is able
to make honey.

There are those that look ahead always without ever
looking back, my father said,
Who, in order to be a human being, must have neither
beggary nor riches,
Setting no store by those outer comforts and those empty
enjoyments which are of no account.

There are too many people that are too worried about
what they are doing and not worried enough about what
they are being, my mother said,
Who, in order to think, must have the noise of words,
Chaining my wild mind like a madman no one can tie
down.

There are few called to enlighten than to shine and to
illuminate than to reflect, my father said,

Who, in order to love living, must learn to love crosses,
Holding virtue to be not so difficult as it is inconvenient.

There are more nails than hammers in the lonely crowd,
my mother said,
Who, in order to fall blindly into the arms of the
uncommitted, must temper community with
individuality, individuality with reason, reason with
instinct, and instinct with passion,
Daring to let go of my mother's hand and walking alone
together through the toy fair.

SANTA, SUPERMAN, AND SIDDHARTHA

Santa Claus is the most important person in my life. He changed me forever. I was a lonely truck driver. I figure I was on the road for five million miles. That was twelve years ago. One day, my head is cold. So I go to the nearest department store and I notice a load of Santa hats. The red kind with the long tail and a big snowball. I pull one on my head and a little boy runs across the store shouting and pointing at me, "It's Santa!" It is like I woke up and everything is perfectly clear to me. My friends are skeptical and some people ask where is my white beard. But the biggest mistake you can make is not believing in yourself. Every morning when I walk through my front door, I am Santa Claus.

Superman is the most important thing in my life. He made me a better man. I was a lonely financial advisor. I figure I invested five hundred million dollars for my clients. That was about twelve years ago. One day, I am eating lunch in a restaurant across the street from my office. I notice that a fat guy sitting a few tables away is choking and gasping for air. He has a big plate of chili peppers in front of him. The red kind with the green stem. So I run across the room and slap him on his back a few times as hard as I can. He coughs up a whole pepper and he stares at me, "Thank you, Superman!" It is like I woke up and I see everything again and again and again for the first time. My friends can be cruel and some of them ask me to bend steel with my bare hands. But for once in my life, I believe in who I am. Every morning when I pull on my red boots, I am Superman.

I ASKED MY EX

And I asked my husband what he wanted me to give him
on his birthday.
He said, "Give back my illusions of you."

And I asked my husband what he wanted from me on our
wedding anniversary.
He said, "Take back my good memories of you."

And I asked my husband what he wanted to be my
Christmas gift to him.
He said, "Go back in time and kick me, beat me, and
abuse me."

And my husband wept in my arms, "It is cruel that I
can remember the past but I cannot change it and that I
cannot remember the future but I can change it."

GOD IS MY FATHER

God is my exaggerated father.
He sits on a great machine.
In his arms, he holds a thermometer, a parachute, an
empty cup, a telephone, and a pair of shoelaces.
In his hands, he holds a red pen and a big black book
with a picture of me on its cover.
In his mind, he is full of wonder.
Why is it just out of her reach?
Why is she postponing the wedding?
Why does it not mean what she thinks it means?
Why would anyone want to be a mother of four?
Why does she need four reasons to leave early?
Why is nothing left of marriage but impediments?
Why does she hate over half of the people she knows?
Why are there four reasons Jesus waits to come back?
In his heart, he weeps for victor and spoils.
Who killed Socrates?
Who voted for Hitler?
Who told her it is easier to marry a rich man she does not
love than to marry a poor man she does?
In his room, there are four pictures in simple wood
frames hanging on the wall above his bed.

THE GOOD MOTHER

My mom loved me with all of her heart,
She would read to me her old letters from dad until I fell
asleep,
Then she would wander outside and sleep in the yard,
But she woke up screaming at sunrise when the
sprinklers turned on,
And she would stagger into the kitchen and try to make
pancakes for me,
But she usually forgot some of the ingredients and they
tasted like wet cardboard,
Once I found a cigarette butt in my waffle but I thought
it was a big chocolate chip and I ate it,
She drove me to school in her pajamas and we sang songs
in the car.
Sometimes she would get sick and I put her to bed with
my unicorn.

THE FUTURE OF THE PAST

I was with a guy for five years. He was much older than me. I tried to end it and he kidnapped me. He tied me down and tattooed his name all over my body. Every time I dress and every time I undress I look at them. And I can feel his body on top of me and feel the needle on my breasts. He owns me. I am his prisoner. I am a captive in my own body.

There were twelve men in my squad in Iraq. That morning we loaded in a vehicle to go on a rescue mission. Someone I never saw before tapped me on the shoulder and told me to move up to the next vehicle. I did as I was ordered and as I sit down I hear a huge explosion. My squad's vehicle got hit. The bomb cut everyone into little pieces. I covered them with blankets so dogs couldn't make a meal of my friend's arm. I am the only guy left to meet with all of their mothers, daughters, girlfriends, and sisters. I had my buddies' names tattooed all over my body. Every time I dress and every time I undress I see them. And I feel the explosion and feel the blanket in my hands. They own me. I belong to them. I am their prisoner. I am what is outside me and what is inside me.

My teacher, Miss O'Sullivan, waited for the rest of the class to leave the room. Then she kissed me on the forehead. My Uncle Duke was sitting in the living room when I got home from school. He said, "Mommy passed away this morning." I looked inside the box, "Where did she go?" "The box is what is inside and what is outside," he said. "Where is the universe?"

THE UNQUALIFIED LIFE

I am a son, father, husband, neighbor, doctor, liar, thief, and adulterer. I watch him in the park that exists across the street that exists from my office that exists. Every morning that exists, he sits on the same bench that exists to play with the children that exist and feed the birds that exist. I have been thinking that he would not be there without me. My father, my daughter, my wife, my friends, my colleagues, my lawyer, and my mistress cannot see me. I have been thinking that I cannot be here without them. I see him and I see the birds and the children and the bench and the park and the street and the office. I see them and I know that they exist. They are qualified. But I cannot see the I that sees them. I cannot find it. I woke up this morning planning to kill myself. Because I do not know what I am looking for. I am not qualified.

ONE CANNOT HAVE THE SAME RELATIONSHIP WITH MOTHER AND FATHER AS WITH A CAB DRIVER

I am seven and my mother and father watch me on television in the studio audience of a children's program. He has a funny name for a clown. It is Hitler. Hitler asks each child, "And what do you want for Christmas?" I say, "I want a new mother and father." I hear a loud and instantaneous gasp. I am weeping.

Our neighbors hear my mother and father fighting as our house does not have conditioned air. Mr. Manson knocks on our front door. My father says, "We are okay, Charles. Thank you." My father and mother say that two of us must live with him and two of us must live with her. They make us take turns picking my mother or my father. This is because we are too many. It is my turn.

My mother is listening to loud music. I say goodbye to my sister and my brother. I sit in the front seat of the car like my mother. My father shakes his fist in front of my face. He says that they are not his children. I love my father and mother. And why I want to kill them.

THE IDEAS BEHIND THE LIES WE BELIEVE

Thus, on being told that Jesus died to pay for my sins . . .
"For that action alone he should be awarded a PHD in accounting."
Thus, on being told by my father that he wants to divorce my mother . . .
"Yes, of course you do. My mother has given everything else to you."
Thus, on being told that my boyfriend has been fucking my best friend . . .
"Nothing is so difficult as not trusting your heart to the one you love."
Thus, on being told by my husband that he doesn't love me anymore . . .
"Now I understand why lions eat lambs."
Thus, on being told by my doctor that my baby will never be the same as other children . . .
"Good."
Thus, on being told that my ex-husband's wife is dying of bone cancer . . .
"She filled a much needed void in my life."
Thus, on being told that my son has died of a drug overdose . . .
"He is proof that intelligent life does exist in the universe."
Thus, on being told that the Bible says it is better for a woman to be a lonely virgin than to be a popular whore . . .
"I don't care what people do in bed as long as it is interesting."

Thus, on being told by my doctor that my breasts do not serve any useful purpose . . .

"Then I will keep them in a jar on my desk."

Thus, on being told that I have about six months to live . . .

"A hunter and a lion were arguing over who is more compassionate. The hunter said, 'I kill for pleasure.' The lion said, 'I kill for food.' Now there was a mighty storm and they took shelter under a tree. But a bolt of lightning hit the tree, utterly destroying it and instantaneously killing both hunter and lion."

THE INSIDE OUTSIDE MAN

He is a fussy man.
A man who shaves twice a day.
He studies maps as he reads novels.
Novels by Thomas Hardy.
He is not a man of his hands.
And the hands that loosen up the car never lay a hand on the engine.

He gives it to me with two hands.
A comb is a fragment of Jesus's cross.
It serves no useful purpose.
A rake is useless in a desert.
It is a statue to his mother who taught him to carry it.
And it pleases his mother to know it is in his pocket.

He wears pants with two back pockets.
Just as causes precede effects.
Thus, he was a boy walking behind a pretty girl.
The girl tripped and fell in a big mud puddle.
He gave her his clean, white handkerchief today.
And will ruthlessly carry it for her tears tomorrow.

He says a father without a pocket knife is not worthy of respect.
Just as we learn to speak without understanding language.

He peels in one, long, thin, red, curling ribbon.
He puts all the true stuff in.
And practices his speech in the bedroom mirror,
"A father is not a father is not a father."
And holds an apple out to me at the end of it.

A BULL, A MATADOR . . . ME

I hope to be able to work at a school. I studied hard to
be a teacher for six years in jail. But I have a boot on my
throat and nobody will give me a chance to work with
human beings.

Lusting bees could do no better than this man. In
my heart he will find a flashlight, an umbrella, and a
parachute.

I am proud of my name. It means "priest." In the
beginning, there once was a holy man in our family. And
as a servant of God, he was required to sacrifice his real
name and become a Khoury.

The merciful bull and arrogant matador could do no
better than this man. In my heart he will find the source
of vanity in an infinite ocean of humility.

As a boy, every Sunday me and my grandfather, Naji,
walked around his neighborhood in Brooklyn. The last
time, he talked about his childhood and about his mother
and about his brothers and sisters and about a girl called
Mary. Then we filled our pockets with stones. And as
we were throwing them at his house and smashing the
windows, he wept.

Abraham Lincoln could do no better than this man. In
my heart he will find the cause of all suffering, the cure
of suffering, and the way to the cure.

IN EVERY MIND ARE THREE PICTURES

She could not sit in a bus without starting a conversation. She knew the name of every person in our neighborhood. She knew the names of all the pizza delivery guys. She knew the names of everybody who worked at her favorite restaurants and everybody in their families. She knew the names of everyone in our church and the names of every doctor and nurse who helped kill her. My mother knew many names. But mom had few friends and her memorial service was empty. My mother was not who she thought she was.

This song means a lot to me. I constantly listened to it during one of the most tragic experiences of my life. My first girlfriend left me for another guy. John and George got so sick of hearing it that they disabled the jukebox. They found a cheap hooker for me and I was fine after a couple of weeks. We broke up but I often think of her and hope she found true happiness. She showed me who I really am. The hooker, I mean.

A woman climbs to heaven and speaks with Jesus. "Who am I?" she asks. "You are not who you think you are and you are not who I think you are. You are the person others think you are," Jesus answers. "But how can I know who that is?" the woman replies. "You must see the world with their eyes and become an object to yourself. Only then will you know who you really are," He says. "And when are you coming, Lord?" "I'm not even excited," Jesus replies.

"CHEERFUL DENIAL IS WARM AND COMFORTING UNTIL ONE FACES THE BETRAYALS THAT ARE NECESSARY TO MAINTAIN IT"

My lap dance is pretty decent. My uniform is a bra, thong, stilettos, heavy eye makeup, and bright red lipstick. They touch my breasts. They spank my ass. They stick a tongue down my throat. I will grind a dick hard for twenty a song but a hand job costs extra. It is a skill like any other. I don't think about things that I don't think about. I plan to quit before my parents come to town for my graduation. I scrub myself ruthlessly in the shower. It is a good story to tell myself to live without shame.

I died in a deep coma from a disease of the brain and woke up in heaven. It looked too real to be unreal. It was filled with beautiful butterflies and souls dancing and riding bicycles and angels with heavy eye makeup and bright red lipstick. What did God look like? He had luscious white hair and a long white beard. He had a hearty laugh and wore red boots. He carried a rock so big that even he could not lift it.

I returned from war to do what I enjoyed. I wandered the streets of my city asking questions and debating answers. I wanted to inspire my neighbors to think and reason for themselves. Like Jesus, I never had a job. Like Santa, I never wrote a book. Like Superman, I never had a big title or a fancy office or a fat paycheck. But my friends loved me and wrote many stories about my life and death.

THREE LESSONS OF LIFE

Lesson 1:

My mother was drunk and we were shopping in an antique store. We found an old oil lamp. It was covered in dust and etched on its side said Made In Iraq. I was rubbing off the dirt when a Genie flew out who looked just like my father. His skull was crushed and he was missing a hand and most of his right leg. The Genie said, "I will give each of you one wish." "Me first!" said my mother. "I wish I could figure out how to be happy without you." The Genie put his hand in his pocket and pulled out a gun. "Put this in your mouth and pull the trigger and you will have your wish," he said. Then he looked at me. And I said, "I wish I was the most beautiful girl in the world, Daddy."

Moral of the story: My memories are like a kingdom as an apple pie is like my mother's suicide.

Lesson 2:

A crow was sitting in a tree and reading a Playboy magazine to a rabbit, "A man was getting in the shower as his wife was finishing her shower when the doorbell rings." Just then a sparrow flying south for the winter fell to the ground. "Only a miracle can save him now," said the rabbit. And they carried the little bird to the wolf who jumped on the sparrow and ate him.

Moral of the story: A family is like a circle as the sun is like a hole in the sky.

Lesson 3:
A priest offered a lift to a Hollywood movie star
who looked just like my mother. "Will you hear my
confession?" asked the movie star. "Yes," said the priest.
An hour later the priest blessed the movie star, "All your
sins are forgiven." A turkey was chatting with a bull in
the back seat of the car. The bull turned to the priest and
said, "There ought to be one sin she never stops paying
for." And the turkey laughed ruthlessly.
Moral of the story: Solipsism is like loneliness as Romeo
and Juliet are like my father and my mother.

THE TIGHTROPE OF PASSING SOMEONE ON THE STREET THAT ONCE WAS A CLOSE FRIEND BUT NOW IS A STRANGER

I wish I missed you.
I should not have fallen for a married man.
You were the kind of person that smiles when you are
caught telling a lie.
You never stopped for a hug and a kiss but passed over
me in silence.
I was always there for you and you were often there
for me.
I remember the last time you made me feel trapped.
You said, "Nobody understands me and I don't
understand myself."
You said, "I have been married for seven years and I am
so alone."
I remember the pain of seeing you holding hands and
sharing a kiss.
I had to feel lost before I could figure out how to get
from nowhere to somewhere.
You said that you feel unwanted, unfulfilled, uncertain,
and unattainable.
You said that you feel empty.
I was deceived by your contradictions and tautologies.

I wish I could talk to someone like me about someone like you.

You knew my room.

I knew only my room.

You told me how lonely you were because you were afraid that you would lose me and you would not have anyone.

I did not tell you how lonely I was because I was afraid that you would leave me and I would not have anyone.

You wanted to be yourself but you were too afraid.

I was too afraid of myself to be what you wanted.

I wish you missed me.

THE MYTH OF THE LITTLE MAN IN THE LITTLE ROOM

What goes on inside him when he thinks about me?
Where does he keep his feelings and thoughts from me?
Why is there the little man in the little room?
Why does the little man keep his thoughts and feelings
about me in the little room?
Why is the little room known only to the little man?
Why can't I know what is in the little room apart from
the little man?
Is there the little room apart from the little man?
Is there the little man apart from the little room?
Why can't I find what is in his little room as I can find
what is in his wife's purse?
Why does the little man keep his thoughts and feelings
about me to himself?
Why are there unthought thoughts and unfelt feelings
lying about in the little room just waiting to be thought
and felt?
Why can he make a mistake and be wrong about what
the little man keeps in the little room?
Does he really love me or is he wrong about what is in
the little room?
What does he mean when he says that he doesn't know
what he wants?
Why can't he find his thoughts and feelings about me in
the little room to think and feel them?
What if he says that he loves me but the little man finds
that he is wrong and he doesn't know it?
What if he says that he doesn't love me but he is wrong?

What if the little man finds that he loves me but he
doesn't find it?
What if the little man is keeping from him how he feels
about me?
What if the little man has mislaid his feelings about me
and he cannot find them?
Why can't the little room be transparent to me?
Why can't I know that he loves me or he know that I
love him?
Why must we play guessing games with the little man in
the little room?
What if we stop playing games?
Do we, then, cease to exist?

NOW I KNOW WHAT IT MEANS TO SEE

I'll let you in on a secret:

Socrates explained nothing.
Wittgenstein described nothing.
Diogenes cured nothing.
Kierkegaard predicted nothing.
Because answers are only real when we experience them
ourselves.

George Washington and I have faith in structures. The
structures of consciousness are the structures of life.
Fathers die before mothers. Husbands before wives. Sons
before daughters. Brothers before sisters. He walked in
from the rain. "Your mother has died," he said. "Yes, she
wanted you to know that she loves you." "But," I said, "I
have no mother?"

Not the deed.
Not the goal.
Not the motivation.
Not the need.
Because the only thing that matters is the spirit in which
something is done.

My wife and child and everyone I love endures the
process of age, disease, and death. All living beings are
prisoners of process. Leadership requires followership.
Umbrellas require rain. Prayers require grief. Cups

require emptiness. He sat in my favorite chair. "Your wife is sleeping in my bed," he said. "Yes, she wants you to know that she does not love you." "But," I said, "I've changed?"

If it sings then it will mourn.
If it stands then it will fall.
If it lives then it will perish.
If it comes together then it will fall apart.
Because the greatest teacher has nothing to teach.

My father is climbing through our kitchen window carrying a pillow case filled with boxes in his arms. The greatest illusion is that I can see through illusions. Love equals vanity. Vanity equals greed. Greed equals compassion. Compassion equals loathing. He put his arms around me. "The operation was a success but your father is dead," he said. "Yes, he spoke of running from the parking lot to the hospital carrying your mother in his arms." "But," I said, "What of Lazarus?"

I HIT MYSELF ON THE HEAD WITH THE BOOK AND I HEARD A HOLLOW SOUND AND THE BOOK WAS NOT EMPTY

I don't want my free sandwich. I want the birthday boy here to have two sandwiches on his special day. It is all I have to give him.

My father got drunk and set my mom on fire. She has big scars on her face. I write her letters To The Most Beautiful Woman In The World. She doesn't know it is me. So she cries as she reads them.

One day I drink only water for get rid of hunger. She gave me her lunch and touched my hand, "Eat."

I don't need to live in a nursing home. I do it just to be with her.

My neighbor beat his dog. I stole him and got arrested. I will never give him back.

She calls me her daughter. My real mother won't talk to me.

I have always been a very tall woman and very
embarrassed by it. I married a guy in a wheelchair
because I love him.

I lost my breasts to cancer. The first time he saw me
without clothes, my husband handed me the love note he
wrote to me in the 6th grade.

10 THINGS I WISH MY ABORTIONIST HAD TOLD ME WHEN I WAS 18

1. Just like any other morning.
2. I sat on his bed and watched.
3. My Uncle Arthur dress for work.
4. His hair was black and shiny and perfect.
5. But this one morning without reason.
6. For the first time in my empty life.
7. I could see that he poked his head.
8. Through the hole in his shirt.
9. Without disturbing a single hair and in a flash.
10. I knew I could walk on water.

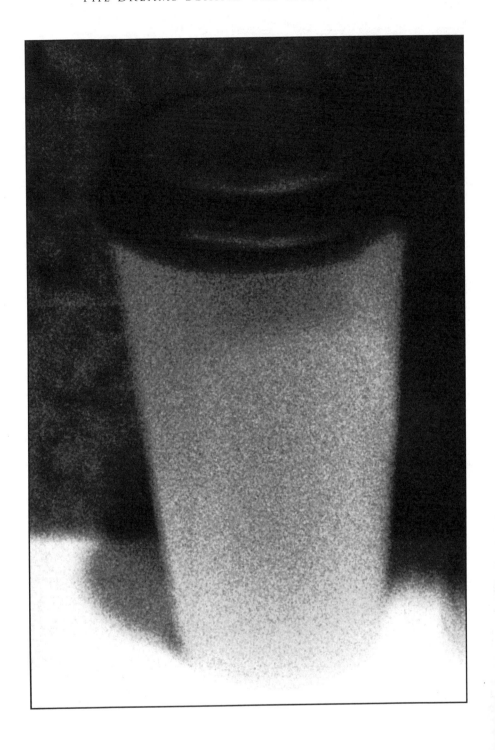

AMEN

My father and I talked
For the last time
At his wedding
I was his Best Man
We had a terrible fight
About his oldest son
And my only brother
On this very day
17 years ago
"Father dying come home brother"
But living walls grow stronger
Neither time nor place bound
In a timeless present
Of a futureless past

THE AUTHOR OF *THE DREAMS BEHIND THE LIES WE LIVE BY*

❧

It has been my good fortune to know Hippolyte Flandrin as scientist and priest, student and professor, bum, and now, poet. At his best, he is a merciless critic of his own past and, says he, a creator of useful toys that only a lucky fool needs or desires. Such as his poetry. Dr. F bounces around the world in pursuit of the source and an infinite ocean of wisdom. He says that he will find it only when he stops looking. If you happen to meet him on the street or find him sleeping in your bed, fear not. For I have seen him both celebrated as a chief cornerstone of social conformity and cursed as a lover of all that is corrupt, blasphemous, and wicked. That tattoo on his left arm may help solve his behavior: "The Individual." He showed it to me, "Did you not know, then, what I am?" I have never known him to tell a lie, but there is no end to his hypocrisy. I have never known him to love the gods, but there is no limit to his kindness. There is no man who has more reason to weep, but I have never known a woman not to weep with him. To befriend him is to be filled both with love and wonder. And whether it is possible to be his friend without becoming selflessly devoted to him, I probably shall never know.

RMKHOURY

Made in the USA
Middletown, DE
11 May 2015